CHINA

Contents

AROUND THE WORLD

Our world has many countries. Each country has beautiful land. It has its own rich history. And, the people have their own languages and ways of life.

China is a country in Asia. What do you know about China? Let's learn more about this place and its story!

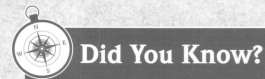
Did You Know?
Mandarin is the official language of China. The words are written in characters.

CHINA

Julie Murray

VISIT US AT
www.abdopublishing.com

Published by ABDO Publishing Company, PO Box 398166, Minneapolis, MN 55439.

Printed in the United States of America, North Mankato, Minnesota.
042013
092013

 PRINTED ON RECYCLED PAPER

Coordinating Series Editor: Rochelle Baltzer
Editor: Sarah Tieck
Contributing Editors: Megan M. Gunderson, Marcia Zappa
Graphic Design: Adam Craven
Cover Photograph: *Shutterstock*: Izmael.
Interior Photographs/Illustrations: *AP Photo*: AP Photo (p. 17), Imaginechina via AP Images (p. 33), Misha Japaridze (p. 19), Lee Jin-man (p. 15), Writer Pictures/wcp via AP Images (p. 31); *Glow Images*: © Eye Ubiquitous (p. 29), © Image Plan/Corbis/Glow Images (p. 21), Juniors Bildarchiv (p. 23), Yvan TRAVERT (p. 27); *iStockphoto*: ©iStockphoto.com/bjdlzx (pp. 5, 34), ©iStockphoto.com/cglade (p. 25), ©iStockphoto.com/cuiphoto (p. 9), ©iStockphoto.com/menabrea (p. 25), ©iStockphoto.com/pengpeng (p. 11); *Shutterstock*: E. Pals (p. 16), Gang Liu (p. 35), Globe Turner (pp. 19, 38), Hung Chung Chih (p. 27), Jakrit Jiraratwaro (p. 21), Roman Sigaev (p. 38), ssguy (p. 34), testing (p. 11), Ian D Walker (p. 13), YANGCHAO (p. 35), Peter Zaharov (p. 37), Jarno Gonzalez Zarraonandia (p. 35).

Country population and area figures taken from the CIA World Factbook.

Library of Congress Control Number: 2013932157

Cataloging-in-Publication Data

Murray, Julie.
China / Julie Murray.
   p. cm. -- (Explore the countries)
ISBN 978-1-61783-807-1 (lib. bdg.)
1. China--Juvenile literature.   I. Title.
951--dc23

2013932157

The famous Great Wall of China stretches thousands of miles.

PASSPORT TO CHINA

China is located in eastern Asia. It has 14 countries on its borders.

China is the fourth-largest country in the world. Its total area is 3,705,407 square miles (9,596,961 sq km). China has the world's largest population! More than 1.3 billion people live there.

WHERE IN THE WORLD?

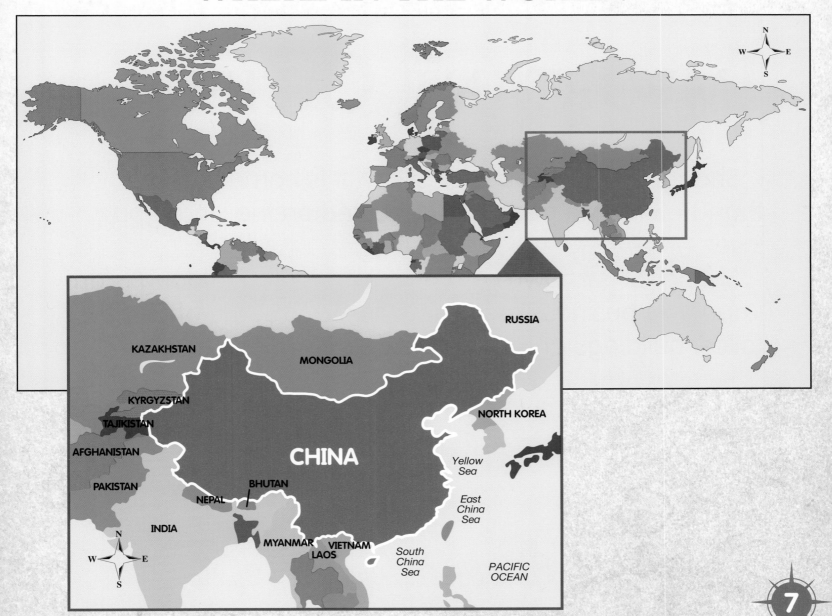

IMPORTANT CITIES

Shanghai is China's largest city. It is home to more than 14.3 million people. It is located on the Huangpu River.

Shanghai is known as a business center. Pudong is an important business area within the city. Some of China's tallest buildings are in this area.

SAY IT

Shanghai
SHANG-heye

Huangpu
HWAHNG-POO

8

Shanghai's Oriental Pearl Tower is 1,535 feet (468 m) tall. It has a restaurant that turns in a circle.

Beijing

CHINA

Chongqing

Shanghai

Beijing is China's **capital** and second-largest city. It has more than 11.5 million people. It is known for its temples, palaces, and stone walls and gates. In 2008, the Summer Olympics were held there.

Chongqing is China's third-largest city, with more than 9.6 million people. This port city is more than 3,000 years old. It is located on the Yangtze River.

SAY IT

Beijing
BAY-JIHNG

Chongqing
CHUNG-CHIHNG

Yangtze
YAHNG-SEE

The Great Hall of the People (*above*) is a government building in Beijing.

Even though Chongqing is an old city, it has many tall buildings.

CHINA IN HISTORY

China has a long history. It was one of the first **civilizations**. Its written history goes back more than 3,500 years! Other great nations took ideas from the Chinese way of life.

For more than 2,000 years, China was ruled by **dynasties**. These include the Qin, Tang, Song, and Ming. **Emperors** led the country. Over the years, other countries tried to take over China. But it remained strong.

Did You Know?

The Chinese made the first paper and compasses. They also came up with a type of writing called calligraphy.

The Forbidden City is a walled area in Beijing. It was the home of China's emperors from 1420 to 1912.

The last Chinese **emperor** gave up power in 1912. This began a period of change.

For many years, **Nationalists** and **Communists** fought to control China. In 1949, the Chinese Communist Party took over. This party controlled the country's **resources** and valued hard work.

Today, China is still ruled by the Communist Party. Government leaders meet in the Great Hall of the People (*below*).

Timeline

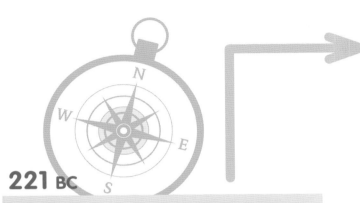

206 BC

The Han Dynasty began its more than 400-year rule. During this time, Chinese traders used the Silk Road to reach Europe. They brought silk west and returned with gold and other goods.

221 BC

The Qin **Dynasty** began ruling China. Its rule lasted about 15 years. It made a standard writing system and standard weights and measures.

AD **618**

The Tang Dynasty began ruling. The time between 618 and 907 was considered a golden age for China. The country became known for its strong arts and military.

1912

The Qing **Dynasty** was overthrown. This ended more than 2,000 years of dynasties serving as China's government.

2013

Elections were held in March. Xi Jinping was chosen as president by the National People's Congress.

1949

The Chinese **Communist** Party won control of the government.

AN IMPORTANT SYMBOL

China's flag was adopted in 1949. It has a red background. There are five yellow stars on its top left corner. The large star stands for the Chinese **Communist** Party. The small stars stand for the people.

China's government is run by members of the Chinese Communist Party. Its groups include the National People's Congress and the State Council. China's president is the chief of state. The premier is the head of government.

The color red is often connected with Communism. This is true in China and other places.

Xi Jinping became the president of China in March 2013.

ACROSS THE LAND

China is known for its mountains, forests, and plains. The Himalaya mountain range is in the southwest. The western part of the country has deserts. Most people live in the plains and **deltas** of eastern China.

China has important waterways. Major rivers include the Yangtze and Huang He. The country is on the Pacific Ocean and can have **typhoons**.

Did You Know?

In January, the average temperature in China ranges from below 0°F (-18°C) to 60°F (16°C). In July, it is about 80°F (27°C) throughout most of China.

The Yangtze is Asia's longest river. It is also the third longest river in the world.

The Himalayas are home to some of the planet's highest peaks.

Many types of animals make their homes in China. These include camels, giant pandas, monkeys, leopards, badgers, yaks, and tigers.

China's land is home to many different plants. These include bamboo plants, larch trees, and peony flowers.

Giant pandas are a type of bear. They eat bamboo.

EARNING A LIVING

China has many important businesses. The country makes goods including cloth, toys, and electronics. Its factories also make car and airplane parts. People work in service jobs, such as helping visitors.

China has many natural **resources**. Its rivers provide water power to make electricity. Iron ore and coal come from its mines. Farmers produce rice, wheat, and potatoes. Ducks, hogs, and fish are raised for food.

Did You Know?

About half of China's people work on farms.

Farmers grow crops on hills using terraced fields.

The Three Gorges Dam on the Yangtze River is the world's largest dam.

LIFE IN CHINA

China's people are known for valuing family and working hard. China is also known for its art and history. This can be seen in its drawings, paintings, **pagodas**, and palaces.

Popular foods in China include rice, noodles, dumplings, vegetables, pork, and poultry. More unusual dishes include flower buds and snake meat! Tea is a favorite drink.

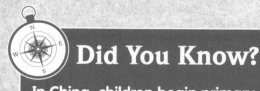

Did You Know?

In China, children begin primary school at age six or seven. Many stop their education after secondary school.

Some older Chinese neighborhoods have narrow streets called *hutongs*.

Long Corridor is a famous walkway in Beijing. It is part of a garden called Summer Palace. It is 2,388 feet (728 m) long and has more than 10,000 paintings!

The Chinese enjoy singing karaoke. Many play card games or a tile game called mah-jongg.

Martial arts, such as tai chi, are popular in China. For these sports, people learn special fighting movements over many years. In this way, they train the mind and the body.

People practice flowing
movements in tai chi.

Famous Faces

China's history is full of strong leaders. Confucius was born in 551 BC in eastern China. His given name was Kongqiu.

Confucius was a teacher. He taught that people should serve others and work hard to be responsible. He died in 479 BC, but people still follow his ideas today.

> **SAY IT**
>
> **Confucius**
> *kuhn-FYOO-shuhs*

30

Confucius was not well known during his life. But after he died, his ideas spread all over the world.

Mao Zedong was born in a small village in southeastern China in 1893. As a student, he saw many changes to China's government.

In the 1940s, Mao led the fight that turned China into a **Communist** country. He was the leader of China from 1949 until 1959. He led the Chinese Communist Party until his death in 1976. As the leader, he told people how to live and work.

Did You Know?

Mao was a writer. For fun, he wrote poetry.

When Mao was China's leader, pictures of him appeared all over China. He was one of the world's most powerful people.

Tour Book

Have you ever been to China? If you visit the country, here are some places to go and things to do!

 ## Remember

See the Tiananmen, or Gate of Heavenly Peace, in Beijing. It was first built in 1417.

Explore

Stroll through Yuyuan Garden in Shanghai. It includes about five acres (2 ha) of buildings and pathways.

 Play

Sled down a sand dune or ride a camel at Crescent Lake. This popular place is in the desert in northwestern China.

See

Visit the Grand Theater in Shanghai. Since opening in 1998, it has been home to shows such as *The Lion King*.

Discover

Look at the faces of about 8,000 terra-cotta warriors. Each one is different! These were buried with an emperor thousands of years ago!

A Great Country

The story of China is important to our world. The people and places that make up this country offer something special. They help make the world a more beautiful, interesting place.

Mount Everest is in the Himalayas, on the border between China and Nepal. At 29,035 feet (8,850 m), it is the highest mountain in the world.

China Up Close

Official Name: Zhonghua Renmin Gongheguo (People's Republic of China)

Flag:

Population (rank): 1,343,239,923 (July 2012 est.) (most-populated country)

Total Area (rank): 3,705,407 square miles (4th largest country)

Capital: Beijing

Official Language: Mandarin

Currency: Yuan

Form of Government: Communist state

National Anthem: "March of the Volunteers"

Important Words

capital a city where government leaders meet.

civilization a well-organized and advanced society.

Communism (KAHM-yuh-nih-zuhm) a form of government in which all or most land and goods are owned by the state. They are then divided among the people based on need.

delta a triangle-shaped piece of land at the mouth of a river. It is made from mud and sand.

dynasty (DEYE-nuh-stee) a powerful group or family that rules for a long time.

emperor the male ruler of an empire.

Nationalist a member of a group that wants to form a separate, independent nation.

pagoda a tower-like temple.

resource a supply of something useful or valued.

typhoon (teye-FOON) a tropical storm that brings heavy rain and wind.

Web Sites

To learn more about China, visit ABDO Publishing Company online. Web sites about China are featured on our Book Links page. These links are routinely monitored and updated to provide the most current information available.

www.abdopublishing.com

Index